"Mommy, Are You Listening?"

By Patrice Lee

Mommy, Are You Listening???
Copyright © 2013 by Patrice Lee
Third Printing - June, 2014

ISBN # 978-0-9837207-6-8

Published by Leep4Joy Books, a Division of
Feinstein Development & Associates
Printed in the USA

Edited by:
Cover Art: Francesco Paolo Ardizonne
Cover Word Placement: Ivory Coast Media

Send all correspondence to:
Feinstein Development and Associates, P.O. Box 48172, Oak Park, MI 48237

Lee has used "author's prerogative" in capitalizing the words "Mom," "Mommy" and "Mommie."

"Mommy, Are You Listening???"

"Mommy, Are You Listening???"

In memory of the sweetest lady I know, my Mom

~ Maxetta M. Fort ~

You're the best Mommie in the world, and a wonderful example of unconditional love, beauty, kindness and grace.

Everything you taught me was honest, pure, lovely and just. Your kindness was genuine, the reflection of a pure heart. To this day, I've not heard a negative word about you. You were genuine.

As a child, I felt I could talk to you about anything. You always made time for me. No matter how busy life got for you, Mom, you always took time to listen. You were there to hear all of my concerns as I poured out my heart to you each day.

Because of you I am a better communicator, speaker and writer. I so miss hearing your sweet voice, your kind words of encouragement, observing your gentle spirit in action. People were drawn to you because of your kindness.

I see the world differently because of you. I'm so thankful to have been able to share 23 years of my life with you, and having you as my Mommie.

I'll always **love** you MOM – **always** {and} forever!

Acknowledgements

~

I'd like to acknowledge and say thank you:

~ Heavenly Father for the inspiration to write and for gifting me with this project.

~ C. Nicole and SAM, for taking the tools that I gave you and applying them to your life. You have made me proud.

~ Francesco Ardizonne, for delivery of my dream cover; it's exactly what I wanted.

~ Mn. Christina Dixon, for your wisdom and insight; and assuring me that this book was needed, now.

~ Silvia Thomas, for your words of encouragement when this book was just a vision in my mind.

~ "Mom" Winans, for seeing value and substance in my material, and for supporting me with your endorsement.

~

I give special thanks to these Moms and Grandmoms for their "Words of Wisdom:"

Mn. Deborah Dixson

"Mommy, Are You Listening???"

Sharon Dumas

Mn. Mary Edwards

Regina Engelhardt

Amina Fakir

Lucille Moore

Gail Perry-Mason

Maeolia Snider

Betty Tanner

Sandra Williams

~

Table of Contents

Endorsement

"A delightful book for Mommies with much needed, Bible-based advice. This, mixed with thought provoking "tweets" about what the babies and children could be thinking on their journey from infancy to adulthood, makes for a very delightful and good read."

Delores "Mom" Winans

"Mommy, Are You Listening???"

Preface

As a young Mom, my desire and my daily prayer was, "Dear God, help me to be the best Mommy I can be." It was such a simple prayer, yet an earnest one; for I depended on Him to help me do it. And I knew that He was helping me, as I watched my children grow.

Motherhood is such a position of honor, yet, serving in the role of a "Mother" can be as grueling an experience as it is noble. For somehow, Moms are expected to work, meet the needs of their family, manage projects, help with homework, keep an orderly house and from babyhood to young adult, present to the world a well-rounded, promising young man or woman.

Sadly, I have observed the gradual decline of the "honor of" and the "respect for" motherhood. Through this observation, I saw a great need for change. This little book came into formation to address that need, in an effort to reach out to mom's everywhere.

The official book of rules for raising a child has never been published, however, each one of us is the offspring of our parent's upbringing, thus, a reflection of the environment of which we were a part.

Of course, your experiences, along with the natural course of life, and the events (planned or unplanned) that occurred along the way, have a lot to do with the changes or adjustments you make to ultimately becoming the person you become. Therefore, you can be a better parent, or in some cases, at least be as good of a parent, as your parents were for you.

Mommy, Are You Listening??? is based on my experience as a Mom, and what worked for me. In no way does it cover the entire scope of motherhood. It does, however, address some of the current trends affecting the very core of motherhood.

We hope this resource will help make the joy of motherhood come together for you as you as you blend the right amount of structure, discipline, faith and love. We know you can do it, but, the key is remaining calm and unnerved through the process.

May you have and enjoy the same peace, beautiful memories, and healthy lifestyle of being a mother as I have, and may all of your needs be met. And know that the rewards will come (later) for all of your "labor of love."

A book created for every woman, color, race, creed, and ethnicity - from all walks of life, because "motherhood" is common ground between us.

Introduction

More than 50 years ago, the role of women - mothers in particular - began to change. They took on more responsibility away from home, while still trying to maintain the routines at home. At first it was a part time job; then, it became full time.

In the beginning of this new work life cycle, it was to help the family have extra money to do more things. The more money Moms and Dads made together, the more things the family needed and wanted. Sadly, the wants began to outweigh the needs, laying the foundation for the "Working Mom."

And households grew from one television to two, from one telephone to multiple phone lines, and from one family car to two or three. Today, it is the expected norm for Moms to work.

Being a working Mom has not only placed extra demands on the family, it has taken its toll on the family unit as a whole. Not only do we have the working wife and mom trying to juggle multiple roles, many Moms are heads of households too.

Although today's Mom spends less time, and has less communication with her child, society still expects this child to be balanced in his thinking, reliable, and to become responsible in all of the affairs of life - and rightly so. After all, children are our future. But, that's a whole lot to expect from a child who has had little to no communication with his Mom, or for the one who comes home alone every day.

Perhaps you've been too busy to pay attention to detail, or were so preoccupied that you haven't heard what your child has been saying to you lately. You could be missing out on some very important information.

Every responsible Mom wants to do a good job of raising her child (children), but, since no one is perfect, she may not always get it right. What is required is that you always do your best, and, with God's help you'll be just fine.

Our goal is to keep you from becoming frustrated with the task of being a Mom, and to encourage you to concentrate on presenting your best gift (a well-rounded individual) to the world.

Congratulations! You're a "MOM"

Quality time spent with your child today will yield tremendous rewards later.

So, You're a Mom? Congratulations!!

To all new Mommy's we say, "Congratulations!" What a privilege to be called "Mom," to be honored with this great responsibility. Whether you've given birth, adopted, or been blessed another way to receive this title, this is one of, if not the most important tasks a woman can have.

You are the first person to have influence on your child's life. You have a chance to make an impression on the world through one precious life. In fact, you can have the greatest influence (impact) on your child's life, if you start early.

If you're like most moms, you'll put your children first and yourself last. And once you become a Mom, your life will never be the same. May this book become a great source of inspiration and encouragement for you to always "be the best Mommy you can be."

So let's get started Mom!

You may already have learned that being a Mom is one of those jobs that doesn't always get a lot of praise. There's not much certainty about the outcome of your responsibilities, the various projects or numerous challenges that come with them. But, one thing is sure; the work must be done.

For as long as you are Mom, you will have thoughts or concerns about the welfare of your child(ren).

Though the "thank you's" may be few in the early years, as your children get older, you will begin to see the fruit of your labor of love. The more diligent you are at the task, the greater the reward.

In fact, you may never feel the true rewards of motherhood until you think the task is over and your children are grown. But, according to all of the Moms who have adult children, myself included, the task of mothering is never really over.

Since attitude has a lot to do with whether or not we succeed in most things, I am quite convinced that attitude will play a major role here as well. While you're devoting a lot of time and effort, remember too, to keep a positive attitude on the Mommie job; and learn from the experience (mistakes) of others. :)

There will always be those opportunities to second guess what you've done so far. And you may have those moments when you're not sure if your child gets what you're trying to teach him.

And at times you may find yourself holding your breath while waiting to see if your son or daughter will have the courage, stamina, and strength to use all that you've been pouring into them to help them get through some of their tests of life. There's always room for doubt: "Did I do enough?" "Have I shared enough?" "Will they be okay?" It comes naturally.

On the Serious Side of Motherhood

You were blessed with the gift of motherhood, but, being a Mom is serious business. And this precious little life now depends on you to nurture, feed, clothe, shelter and keep him (her) safe from everything that is not good (all the evil forces) in this world.

You are the first expression of love, the first example of good, the evidence of kindness, the voice of justice, the mind of good thoughts and the action figure of good deeds. You must be that tower of strength, and the one who exhibits self-control through all of the trials, disappointments and adversities of life.

You must be able to endure longer days and longer nights. Your opinions, at least for awhile, are not relevant, but your words and actions are. In fact, your kind words and tone of voice, or lack of same, are a reflection of God's love, or not.

Your child will need love, structure and discipline. Love is always most welcome, while structure and discipline - depending on how soon you introduce it - can sometimes be more difficult. The child who receives discipline and structure early in life learns to respect authority, is less likely to be unruly in class, or lack self-control. Introduce them early. :) And make it your goal to have the greatest influence on your child's life in a positive way.

Your Babies and Children – Your Gifts

Perhaps the best way to let your children know that you love them is to tell them and show them often. Many times Moms feel the need to buy the latest clothes, technology or fads to express the love that they have for their children.

But, if you love your children, tell them; and let love be displayed in all of your actions, including and especially in the area of discipline. Unconditional love yields great rewards, at every age.

I chose to raise my children in the fear and admonition of the Lord, and I'm glad I did. Because children go back to what they've been taught over time.

In fact, they not only go back to their roots, sometimes they correct you when they see you deviate from what they know is right. One case in point: I remember when my son was about 5 or 6 years old, we were dangerously cut off in traffic by a fairly rude (very rude) driver. I was not very happy about it and referred to that person as an "idiot." Very quickly (but with respect), my son said, "Mom, that wasn't nice. You shouldn't say that."

Boy, did I feel guilty. But, at the same time, I also felt proud. He was aware of appropriate behavior versus less than the best, and was willing to take a stand for what was right. And, as children will do, he spoke the truth out loud, but in a very respectful way. He recognized good versus evil to put it bluntly.

My son was putting into practice - or at least reminding me of what he had been taught - to walk-in-love, agape love (the God-kind of love) with my fellow man. I had let the other driver upset me and was not able to contain my disappointment, after a very long day at work.

It was this conversation, along with many others, that I realized how important my actions and reactions were in the life of my children; for no matter what I did in life, I clearly understood that my character influenced the development of my children's character. This is an area that is so often ignored or overlooked.

After that incident in the car with my son, I very quickly pulled myself together. I returned to my quiet state of happiness, for "pleasant" was how I wanted to be at all times.

Let's define "pleasant" as "a quiet state of happiness." :)

~

A Special "Mommie" note: Your child is a most precious gift from God. How are you taking care of your most precious gift? If you're multi-tasking, are you multi-tasking at your child's expense? And when you are in the presence of your child, could anything be more important than tending to his/her needs at that moment? ... at any moment?

~

"Mommie, Do You Have to **Work?**"

Don't forget!!!

Your first job is the most important one.

There's No One Like You Mommie

Baby Talk: If your baby could talk, here's what your baby might say:

"When I first got here Mommie, I didn't have to make much noise for you to see about me. You checked on me every 10 minutes to see if I was wet, needed to be turned, or make sure I was still asleep. If I twisted or turned you were right there to check on me.

I didn't get to exercise my lungs very much, because you didn't want to hear me cry. You talked to me, smiled at me, and you spoke the kindest words. You talked to me when I was awake, until I fell asleep. You really talked a lot. :)

As the weeks went by, you gave me a chance to exercise my lungs a bit more. You even let me twist and turn a little, as my newness wore off and you needed more rest, 'cause it had been a while since you had a full night's sleep.

As I grew a little older, you let others take me from time to time. In fact, sometimes I didn't see you all day, because you had a job away from home too. At first, someone would come in to take care of me at home, but later you dropped me off at these very big places, with many other children and lots of unfamiliar faces.

I didn't like it at first, because I was still adjusting to being here - outside of your safety net, in the tiny crevices of your womb. In fact, you had everything I needed. God gave it to you naturally. Besides, nobody could care for me like you.

But, I had to learn very quickly to adapt to each new face, and all the changes taking place in my life. For now when I cry no one comes to check on me. No one cares if I'm really wet or full of number two. Mommie, no one cares for me the way you do.

Will there be any one in this place to help me tie my shoes (when that time comes)?   'Cause everyone here is busy Mommy, busy, just like you."

Your baby

"MOMMIE" NOTE: Sometime Mommies get so busy that everything has to wait, including their babies and children. But, whenever you are at home with your child, could anything be more important than tending to the needs of your child - a wet diaper/a hungry child - at that moment? ... at any moment?

The "Working" Mom

Being a "Mommie" is both
a "work of art" and a "labor of love"

So You Have to Work?

There used to be a time that if you were a working Mom, it was because you chose to work. There was also a time that a Mom might decide to work after her youngest child was in school. That is not the case today.

You might be surprised to know that when God made Adam, and formed Eve from his side, it was His divine plan for Adam to take care of his family. This meant Adam would protect and make sure Eve had everything she needed for comfort. Eve, was designed to be Adam's helpmate. So, Adam tilled the ground, named the animals, and was responsible for protecting and caring for that which belonged to him - his family.

When they disobeyed God in the Garden of Eden, everything changed. And sin destroyed God's perfect plan for man. As the sin nature of man in this world has increased, men continue to work hard and harder, but women have also joined the workforce. As society has progressed and moved further from God's perfect plan for man, women have begun to work as hard as men, sometimes competing for their positions – positions once considered a man's job.

Caught-up, in the Workplace

Today, work away from home is no longer considered a man's job, and most working, expectant (expecting) Moms, continue working up to the date of, or within a few days of delivery, if there are no complications during their pregnancy. These same Moms return to work within six weeks of the birth of their child. And this has become the expected norm.

As this bounce-back-to-work lifestyle became the accepted norm, over 40 years ago, we began to witness the decline of the meaning of motherhood, and parenting as our society once knew it. And the way our parents and grandparents understood parenting and motherhood to be has now become a thing of the past.

Fast forward to the 21st century: Today, as we look at our children and youth, we are asking ourselves, "What happened?"

Of course, there are so many other factors that have contributed to the decline of quality living and wholesome family life. But we'll stick to "Mommy business."

Let's look at the stats and see where we are.

Working Mom, You Are Not Alone

Today, there are more "working Moms" outside of the home, than "non-working" Moms at home. Let's look at the working Mommy Stats below:

Working Mommy Stats:

- 61% of all working Moms work away from home
- 86% of Moms surveyed say they are stressed
- 40% of Moms say they always feel rushed

- 85% of working Moms say they are happy
- 80% of stay-at-home Moms say they are happy
- 66% of mothers 17 years or younger work part/full-time jobs

- 62% of working Moms prefer to work part-time

According to public opinion:

- 42 % say a Mom shouldn't work
- 40% feel it's ok for Moms to work part time
- 12% feel that it's ok for a mother to work full time

And when you work, sometimes you just need a little help. Don't worry, because . . .

http://www.statisticbrain.com/african-american-stats/

It's Okay to Call for Help–
. . .Help is on the Way!

Whether you are a working Mom or a stay-at-home Mom, it's okay to call for help. And you may get the help you need from an older child, for children can be taught many values through helping out at home.

Sometimes those lessons come through the discipline of chores, just because it's the right thing to do. Chores help children and teens become responsible.

When the children are very young, you can use the excitement of a new baby brother or sister as a way to introduce some light chores. For example, the older sibling or toddler can help with little things that make a big difference, like handing you a diaper or baby wipes when needed.

This doesn't mean you should take advantage of your older children, but it helps them to understand the principle of teamwork, and the importance of working together as a team. After all, the family unit is a team. And the more each member does their share, the less pressure on you.

So, why not use the help you've got. Let the things your children do become a learning experience in some creative way. This will make it more interesting. Yes, chores can be a pleasant experience too. You can also let them be creative with new ways of doing things and also encourage them to share new ideas as they get older.

Maybe you will want to give an incentive to the child that does chores without being reminded. You can be creative too. Now, do we need to discuss an allowance for each child? Some parents believe in giving an allowance and some do not. I will remain silent on this one. It's your call; but if an allowance is given, you can teach your child to budget, to learn to save, or to spend money wisely, etc. :)

One of the keys to being a successful working Mom is finding ways to get the job done (at home) without being stressed. And if Dad is working and you don't have an older child to assist you, you may need to call for reliable help from another adult as needed.

You never want to feel overwhelmed at home. This is the one place that working Moms need to have peace and comfort.

Let God's peace keep your heart and mind at ease.

Five Steps to Avoid **"Burn-Out"**

For the super busy Moms

"Happiness" is 'joy bouncing around on the inside.'

Be Happy!!!

Step 1: Begin Each Day with a **Grateful Heart**

Be thankful for each new day. What a blessing to be able to wake up, to be able to see this beautiful new day. . . Being grateful for the little things, a great start. You feel better when you wake up happy. Your happy disposition can be contagious to those around you.

Choose this side of happy. Let the spirit of happiness keep you in a healthy state of mind, feeling good from the inside-out. Yes, happiness will keep you carefree.

That's what God wants for you - for all of us – to be carefree, for He gives instruction in His Word to "Cast all of our care upon Him," because He cares for us. He genuinely cares so much about us. (Reference: 1 Peter 5:7)

You don't have to sweat the small stuff. God can handle that too. And His peace will sustain you. Know that He wants to hear from you and desires to be your friend. Seeking Him early each day will give you wisdom. Happiness will continue from day-to-day if you let God handle all of the details.

Note of caution: If you choose to be angry, bitter, or sad, or anything other than happy, your family will be affected by that disposition as well.

"Seek ye first the Kingdom of God, ..." (Matthew 6:33).
"A merry heart doeth good like a medicine. . ." (Proverbs 17:22).

Step 2: Do a Self-Examination

Ask Yourself

Is this a priority? Can the task I'm working on wait until tomorrow? Should I be doing something more important? What needs to be completed today? Do I have time for social media?

If you find yourself going in circles, you may need to re-evaluate your priorities, and ask yourself, "Who's in control?" Is social media taking a big chunk of your day? or other people? It takes discipline to separate from both. Remember, Mom, you are not in control if you're reacting to everything happening around you.

Examining Self

Self-examinations should be done as often as needed, and from time-to-time to determine where you are. As you do the self-examination, you may find that many of the things you've been working on can wait.

Examine your routine. How are you spending your time? What can you do differently? Is there some activity you can eliminate temporarily?   Is there anything that can possibly wait until tomorrow? There's more. . .

Examine all activities from "sun-up" to "sun-down." It might be a good idea to write everything down. Be sure to record everything, so you can have an accurate assessment of your activities.

You may find that you're doing the same thing every day, at the same time – like clockwork – that nothing changes from day-to-day. This is especially true for Moms who work outside of their home. If it's working for you, that's wonderful.

You may observe that every day is different, if you work from home. Your day may be a combination of any of the following: meetings, conference calls, and getting from one appointment to another, while juggling the responsibilities of work and home.

~

One thing in life is certain; there will always be something to do. However, it is the order in which you choose to do it, that can make the difference between peace and chaos.

~

Step 3: Take Time to Plan Your Day!
~ 5 minutes of planning can save hours of wasted time ~

If you want to have a more productive day, you will need a plan. A plan allows you to see your vision on paper and gives you a sense of accomplishment, as you cross each completed task off the list. It sounds so simple, yet, it may not be so easy for the creative person. However, it's a no-brainer for those who think that way automatically.

Whether you are a stay-at-home Mom, or a career Mom/business owner, you need a plan, even when you're at home with your children. This includes evenings, or after work hours, and weekends. It keeps you organized. Their lives and your time are that important and valuable.

It is similar to running your business. In order to be successful at any business, you must have a plan. You may have to revise it often, as your goals change. But, having one will allow for better time management, which is necessary for a stress-free life.

Everything you do, during the course of the day, involves time. The time factor will never go away. Therefore, it will help to manage your time wisely. As you do, things, and life in general, will seem to be in control.

In the previous chapter you were asked to do self-examinations and to record the data. Now that you have documented your routines and assessed your daily activities, you will need to rank them in order to determine which task or activity is a priority, beginning with the number (#) 1, as of most importance.

Once activities are in rank order, decide how much time is needed to complete each task. The more realistic your time denominations, the greater the success rate for task completion, and the better you will feel.

There's a lot of room for flexibility, if your activities are not appointment driven, classes, or meetings. These tend to confine you to a particular day and/or hour of the week. As you perfect your ability to manage time, you will find creative ways to work around them and get it all done.

Now, with each priority numbered, fill in the days and hours of the week on your personal calendar that you plan to get it done. You may not be able to get everything done in that one day, but it will be wonderful to see all that you can accomplish in that one day.

Next, keep this list visible so that you can:
1. Work on each task in rank order of importance. (Hint: I find that it's better to do the most difficult task earlier in the day.)

2. Be sure to work timely and stay on schedule. If you find that not enough time has been given to complete a task, adjustments can be made to allow for task completion. Sometimes there are hidden variables that you didn't anticipate. And some things just take more time.

3. Check off each task as you complete it throughout the day.

4. Manage break times – you need and deserve to take a break like everyone else. Include a five-minute break in-between each task. You can take a brisk walk, or give yourself a facial. ☺

Plan your days off too. You will find that with a plan you can do more things in less time.

Traditionally, we used Saturday or Sunday as our day of rest, and a time for family to spend together in worship and reverent activity. Either day is still a wonderful time for strengthening, restoration and relaxation.

Always, always look forward to the day when you're able to complete everything on your list. When that day comes, cherish it. You'll sleep really well that night. :) . . .and it will be a sweet sleep.

Ask God for guidance as you plan your day. He would be honored to assist you.

The plan is the easy part, because it's what you desire to accomplish. Sticking to the plan is where you may encounter challenges, for it requires discipline to execute the plan.

"Write the vision, and make it plain. . ."

(Habakkuk 2:2b)

Step 4: "LISTEN"

To your inner spirit

Have you been too busy to think lately? If you are too busy to think about things, then you probably have less time to listen, or no time at all. Perhaps you need to slow down. Please stop long enough to hear what is being said.

Since we have your attention, listen to your heart. What comes to mind? What is your spirit saying? Keep every good thought you've been thinking. Focus on the great ideas that God has put in you to do. As you sharpen your listening skills, you'll welcome more creative thought.

Quiet time allows for inner communication to take place in the heart, mind and spirit. The more quiet time you allow self to have, the more peaceful your state of mind.

Now that you have a daily plan, you can schedule time to do other things moderately. You may not always have time for everyone who is vying for your attention on the same day. But, be courteous enough to let them know that you'll get back with them at a later time.

Listen, so you can hear what your inner spirit is saying. Sometimes new ideas surface in those moments when everything around you is quiet and still.

Prescription: Take five minutes every day, once, twice, or as often as you need, to be quiet (and listen).

Step 5: Take **Time Out for You**
Vacation time /Regular Time-outs

Break time must be incorporated into your daily life. And you deserve a break every day. It helps you maintain balance and breaks up the monotony of routine tasks. It's as important to take regular time-outs as it is to plan for a vacation.

Vacation is important and necessary, because it allows you to:

1. Have time for fun; to enjoy life

2. To get away; to rest

3. To take personal time away from the routine

4. To relax, unwind and just do nothing

Vacation is a time to rest and relax; a time to be refreshed and restored, in mind, body and spirit. You can have vacation for five hours or five days, two weeks or two months, if your budget allows for it. Everyone needs a vacation from life's routines. Vacations have been known to improve one's health and one's quality of life.

You may feel that you can't afford it. Well, you may not be able to afford your dream vacation, but you still need to take some time out. After all, how much money does it take to rest, relax, and rekindle your happy state of mind?

A vacation can be a minimal to luxurious expense. It is not so important how much you spend. What matters more is that you take this time out to rest, relax and have fun. Let's break it down a little more.

Many times, particularly if you're a little stressed, it may take awhile for you to feel rested. And you can't really begin to relax until you're fully rested. The two feed off of each other. Therefore, you need enough time on your vacation to do both.

For the family on a small to zero budget, you can have a wonderful picnic in the back yard, at a park, sit on the lake and observe the sunrise or set, watch a cruiser go by or observe the geese as they gather around the pond. Plan a weekend of nothing but fun things to do, at home or whatever local destination makes you happy. If it's in your budget, do it!

When you work hard, you deserve a break from work. Little breaks allow for time to reflect.

Special Note: A good night's sleep can be like a mini-vacation. Both you and your children will reap the benefits of being well-rested, but, you may have to put the children to bed earlier to get the rest you need. And when your child is ready to talk, you'll be ready to listen. . .

"Mommie, may I talk to you?"

Unexpected **"Tweets"**

A tweet that's "short" and "sweet."

Baby "Tweets"
(from a 6 month old)

If your infant baby could tweet you, what would your baby tweet? Let's start with the food.

"It's All About the Food" Tweets:

"Mommie, I'm hungry. Are you?"
"Thank you for breakfast, lunch and dinner." :)
"Do we have any snacks? I'm still hungry."
"Spinach and carrots? Sorry Mommie, I'm full." :)
"This is what I had yesterday. Is there anything else?"
"No beets for me today peeeease." :(
"When I grow up, I'm having desert too?"
"Oh no, . . .not those peas again!" :(
"May I have plums instead of pears?"
"I'll have this later, please. I'm ready for desert."

"Diaper Control" Tweets:

"It's been awhile since you changed me. I'm sure you'll get my drift. . ."
"If I have prunes today, I'm sure I'll lose control."
"I'm not finished yet. Can you change me later?"
"It's more than just a number one, and my diaper is soppy wet." :(

"About Those Colors" Tweets:

(From your baby girl) "Does the rainbow have any other color besides pink? That's the only color I see when I look in the mirror." :(

51

(From your baby boy) "I wore blue yesterday and the day before. Is there any other color besides blue?"

"Time to Get Some Rest" Tweets:

"I love you Mommie. Good night."

"Mommie, shouldn't you go to bed now, cuz I'm gettin' up very early in the morning?" :)

Ps. "I'll wake you up about 2:00a.m. okay? Until then, rest well."

Pps. "You're the best Mommie in the whole world." :)

If Your Toddler Could Tweet . . .
What would your toddler have to say?

"Toddler" Tweets:

"Please don't ignore this little person that you see. At my tender age I need to talk to you, and for you to talk to me."

.

"Oh Mommie, are you listening? Do you understand me when I speak? I'm hurting on the inside, and I can't go back to sleep."

.

"Mommie, I don't mean to bother you. But, I'm hungry. Are you almost through?"

.

"I just wanna know are you okay? You've been busy, almost all day."

.

"I love you so much Mommie. What can I help you do? Maybe I can do dishes, or help with you with the food?"

.

"Let's eat! Hurry, before that cell phone rings (again)."

.

"Mom I don't want anything. I just want to tell you how much I love you. And, can I get a hug too?"

.

"I'm finished. Can you flush it for me please? (yelling) M-o-m-m-i-e, I-'m f-i-n-i-s-h-e-d!!!"

.

"Thank you for listening. It's so nice to know you care. Can we spend more time together tomorrow?"

.

(@ 5:00a.m.) "Wake-Up Mommie! It's a brand new day. It's a happy morning and I want to go out and play."

Oh No, Not That Cyberspace Again:

"I want to play with you Mommie. You've been on 'placebook' all day."

.

"Hey! That's my picture? Did you get permission to put it on the intanet?"

.

"If you don't protect me from the world, who will?"

.

"Grand Mommy puts my pictures in her photo album. Do you know what a real photo album is?"

.

"Mommie, can you put 'place book' away and play with me, p-w-e-a-s-e?"

It's All about Love:

"May I have another hug? I've been waiting for one all week."

.

"Thank you Mommie for loving me the way you do. I love you too."

.

"Mommie, if you talk to me now - while I'm two or three - I'll grow up to make you very proud of me."

.

"Mommie, I love you with all of my heart! And I know you love me, 'cause you told me yesterday."

.

"You are the best Mom in the whole world." :)

.

"I love you Mommie, more than you'll ever know."

Just one more "tweet:"

"Mommie R U test and driben?"

(text and driving) ☺

Sincere **"Tweets"**

~ Straight from the Heart ~

Teary-eyed Tweets: "Mommie, can you hear me? Oh Mommie, did you hear anything I said today?"

"Mommie, Are You Listening?"
(Tweets from a 1st grader)

"Are you listening Mommie? Do you hear the words I say? I just want to talk to you. I don't want to go out and play."

Are you too busy for us to talk today?
And after we talk, maybe could we pray?

"Are you busy Mommie? Do you have some time for me? I want you to know I love you, and I need you. Can't you see?"

"I had a fall at school, and I really hurt my knee Can you look at it when you have the time, and take me to the doctor, please?"

"I'm feeling better now. May I do something nice for you? I can wash dishes or sweep the floor, or help you find your shoe."

"I love you Mommie."

"Mommie" Note: Young children are content if they are given the assurance of your love and their basic needs are comfortably met. Talking to them, listening and showing an interest in their concerns, is vital to their well-being. A Mom should never be too busy to meet her child's needs. No matter how old they get, a child still needs your love. Your time is an expression of love.

If Your Child Could Tweet You, What Would Your Child Say? (from a 3rd grader)

"Mom, is it as hard to be an adult as it to be a child? I had a tough day."

"Mommie, do you love me as much I love you?"

"You promised to take me to the park (two weeks ago). Can we go today? Please??"

"Wonder what life was like when you were my age? Was it this hard?"

About your behavior lately: I don't like what cyberspace is doing to me?

"Can you take me off of Face Book!! Those are not my friends."

"Please don't put this picture on Facebook. The world's been kind of tough on us (children) lately."

"Mommie may I put this picture of you on Face Book? The one that you don't like."

"You used to store our pictures in a real album, now they're all on FB. What happened?"

"I don't want my picture on Face Book today, or tomorrow either for that matter."

"Mommie" Note: Children usually express how they feel. At this age, they are quite open and honest, if their parents have created an atmosphere which welcomes open communication. Let them talk. (Respectfully)

"Mommie, **R U Listening?**"

(From the heart of a fifth grader)

"Mommie can you hear me? I have something to say. I need to know, Did you hear me yesterday?"

"I'm having trouble, and don't know what to do. All the children laugh at me every day at school."

"The teacher doesn't do anything. It's as if she doesn't hear. I'm scared. . . .and I'm trying hard not to to fear."

"Please, can you help me? Mommie? Don't know what else to do. All I know is I've had it. So, please, please don't make me go back to school."

"Mommie, can you help me? I feel like I'm gonna choke. I've got to get away from there, 'cause I'm the brunt of every joke."

"Mommie, are you listening? I have so much more to say. Need to talk to you, before I go to school today. Help me Mommie!! Please find a way."

(Your fifth grader)

A Plea from a Mother's Teen

Mom, are you listening?
Can you hear me when I say
I really need to talk to you.
Will you have some time today?

Why these little things are bothering me
I just don't understand.
It all seemed to happen suddenly.
Can you please give me a hand?

Hey Mom, I know you're busy now,
But, you'd better hurry fast.
'Cause I've been feeling rather strange
Not sure my strength is gonna' last.

Right now, I'd settle for a hug
And a compliment or two,
For there's no doubt that you love me,
But, I just need to talk to you.

"Mommie" Note: Sometimes teenagers don't always say what or how they are feeling. If verbal expression is limited, find a way to open the channel of communication. Do something they like to do – an activity, a sport, etc. And have casual conversation.

Time to Pay Attention Mom!!

Sometimes your child says nothing
At times, he can only look,
For the answers to all of his questions
Can't be found in any book.

Your time, your love, your sacrifice
From all those other things
A warm embrace, and loving smile,
Who knew the peace it would bring.

You can have every kind of technology,
And all the latest stuff,
But nothing can replace a mother's love,
Her smile, embrace, her touch.

"Mommy" Note: I found that when I met all of my children's basic needs and gave them strong spiritual guidance, that the latest designer trends were never an issue for us. More importantly, they were content.

What Do I Do If Trouble Comes?

Many of the problems in society like crime, violence, homicides and other offences are committed by our youth. Even more horrifying today is the disregard for life, to the point that our 6 and 7 year old babies and youths are committing suicide, with more than half of them being a result of or related to bullying.

Children need to talk, and they need someone to listen. But, children are a reflection of their home environment – great parent, great child. On the other hand, if there's a cruel parent, a cruel child with bully-like tendencies, may surface at school and elsewhere as a result of the home environment.

Thus, the term "kinship bully," accurately describes (depicts) the behavior of a cruel parent or a mean-spirited sibling. In fact, some of our youth are mirror images of what is happening in front of them on a daily basis, of both positive and negative influences.

These are some of the things that invite trouble. And, if trouble comes, you must change the way you do things, and be willing to keep making changes until you get the results you desire to have. A loving child is one who is shown love. And a happy child comes from a pleasant environment where his/her needs are met.

Bullies Are Real People

Children are a work of art. Sometimes the art is in rare form, and the labor is long.

Bullies Are Real, but. . .

Since there is so much talk about bullies and so many conversations that feed into it on a daily basis, but even more importantly, since children, youth and young adults are now taking their lives in alarming numbers on a daily basis, we must address it.

Bullies are real, but every mean act or mean thing that a person does is not bullying. Just because someone licks out their tongue, is rude, or laughs at something you do, doesn't mean they are a bully.

All mean-spirited people are not necessarily bullies, but, bullies are usually mean-spirited. However, each circumstance will yield its' own definition based on the person's involved.

If it does happen, your child needs to talk. Will you be there to hear what your son or daughter has to say? And will you make yourself available to listen every day?

Teach and show them love. Love never fails. So let's love one another.

Perfect love leaves no room for fear.

About Those Bullies:

Bullies have been around for a long time.

A "bully" doesn't just happen, and a bully doesn't pop up suddenly or appear out of nowhere. Bullies are created. Very few are born with a mean spirit.

Many are themselves victims of some form of cruel treatment. Others may simply have an insatiable desire to be loved by their Mom and Dad. On the next few pages we will look at some ways in which the character of a bully can be created.

Maybe the child has an older brother or sister who is always picking on them – one who is mean in every way; or perhaps they have a parent who never shows love. Let's take a look at the older sibling.

The older sibling even goes so far as to get the younger sibling in trouble and they haven't done anything. It could be that they are jealous or envious of their younger brother or sister. The older sibling may feel that their sibling gets too much attention, or has too many privileges.

If this behavior continues to go uncorrected, the younger child will do one of two things – retaliate or internalize it. If the child retaliates, it would more than likely be at school, because he or she may feel trapped at home.

This young child may be ignored at first, because their unseemly behavior is not natural. But, after a while it could become the norm, thus the term "bully" becomes attached to his name.

What happened? The child has built up anger over time and the anger has metastasized to a destructive, disruptive eruption on the inside which comes out as abruptly as it feels. So where does the child release it? At school, or wherever they spend most of their time.

What can a Mom do? One of the most important things you can do here is talk to your child. If you don't have talks or converse on a regular basis, the best thing to do is start talking before a crisis arises.

Children are little people who need to express their feelings just like adults need to express their feelings. You may not be able to be your child's best friend, but your child needs to know that they have a friend in you. When your child opens up to you, respond in a most loving manner and be patient enough to let your child share what's on their heart.

And sometimes the child or teen just needs "love," unconditional love. There is no replacement for a mother or father's love. If you're raised in a home without love, you may not be able to walk in such a loving way with others.

Because children (their actions and reactions) are the by-product (result from) of their environment, one of the greatest things a parent can do is love them and teach them how to walk in loving way by example. Kind words spoken, words of praise for good behavior, reassurance of a mother and father's love, produces a good natured, loving and confident child. These children tend to smile more, and are pleasant to be around.

Unfortunately, the child who receives just the opposite, is usually a misguided, troubled child; and there is usually not a good exchange of communication with others. However, there are exceptions to both scenarios.

Now let's get back to the bully and the affects of the bully's behavior. The bully's comments, gestures or threats affect your emotions. When an unkind word or statement is made about you continually, it begins to affect how you feel and can weigh heavily on your thoughts, making it necessary for a release of some sort, i.e., a verbal exchange.

Just like the foods that you put in your body, what goes in, must eventually come out. Our body takes in what it needs, and at some point after the food is digested, the body must release what is not needed to make room for more food. But, the food must be digested first.

Now the parallel is this. When you eat foods that are healthy and nutritious, the results will produce healthy and strong bodies. Foods that are not good for us, over time, will cause our bodies to decay prematurely. Now, it might take 20 or 30 years, but it will show up eventually. Either way, whether we eat healthy or unhealthy, there will be a release.

Notice that illness or disease is not usually right away, but, sometimes a particular food or meal may not be agreeable to the stomach and there is an immediate release. I'm sure you get the picture. :0

So is the case with children, teens and people in general. Most can tolerate considerable teasing for a while, but over time it wears on them, and emotions kick in. Yet, there are some who can't tolerate it, not even for a short duration. Therefore, it is crucial that these individuals be identified immediately.

There will be warning signs to help you identify a child who is being affected negatively as a result of being bullied. Look for the warning signs and move quickly to bring resolve, restoration and support.

Here are some signs you can look for in your child's behavior or demeanor. Your child:

1. Does not want to go to school.
2. Has a loss of appetite or change in eating habits.

3. Has a sudden change in personality.
4. Desires to be left alone; isolates himself/herself
5. Suddenly, your child is irritable most of the time
6. Has a change in sleeping habits, i.e., wakes up every few hours, or doesn't sleep at all.
7. A mild-mannered child may suddenly become disruptive at school.
8. Once a good communicator may give unusual responses to your inquiries, or none at all.
9. Your child may become explosive or overwhelmed with emotion
10. May have a change in posture, from good to a somewhat slouched stance.

If you notice two or more of these signs, start a conversation and keep the channels of communication open by:

1. Showing your support
2. Moving quickly to bring a resolution to the matter.
3. Getting counseling if needed.
4. Staying on top of it until the bullying stops.

Bullied To Death . . .

Bullies have been around for a very long time. Did you know that bullying began with Cain and Abel, the first natural children born into this world?

Do you know the story of David and Saul? When David was a very young man, he had to hide from King Saul to save his life, because this reigning king was very jealous of him and tried to kill David.

Then there was Haman, who hated Queen Esther and all of her people; and Saul-who persecuted Christians-who later became Apostle Paul.

But Jesus, our loving Saviour, endured more bullying than anyone has ever encountered. In fact, his bullies crucified Him, after they laughed at him, betrayed Him, talked about, scorned, ridiculed, then beat Him until the flesh fell off of His back; placing a crown of many thorns onto His head.

They punched Him, kicked Him, broke His bones, and nailed Him to the cross. And He never said a word against them, but asked that they be forgiven. Although He had done nothing wrong, He endured the pain and suffering. He took all of this for **you and me**. Jesus displayed the perfect love of the Father for you to have eternal life. If you haven't made Jesus Lord of your life, invite Him into your heart today.

Those Daily Discussions

How well do you know your children?
Do you have meaningful discussions every day?
Are you teaching them what they need to know?
Have you told them, Jesus is the way?
Are you pointing them in the right direction?
And encouraging them to go?

Do they know that Jesus is coming?
Are they ready for His return?
Can you help them understand?
While there's a deep desire to learn?

"Love," Ethics, Rules and More . . .

"Mom, Did You Forget to Tell Me About ...?"
"Jesus" - Tweets

"Mommie, who is Jesus?"

"Is He someone I need to know?"

"Can you tell me more about Him?

And point the way to go? Please, Mommie!

My heart is open. Do you think He'll speak to me?"

"Love," Rules, Ethics and More

Quality time, strong ethics, and a clean and safe home environment, mixed with **a whole lot of love, will produce a responsible, respectable and loving human being.** And that's what the world needs -- "love."

All children need rules at home, for home is where the standards for life are set. Standards must be established early in a child's life for least resistance. For example, the youth or young adult who is raised in a home without well-defined rules or guidelines is one who will be resistant to authority in the dorm, at school, on the job, and - in the real world – the law.

~ Establish rules for your family and stick to them ~
(. . .because you are preparing your child for life)

As a parent I've learned that:

Children need and respond favorably to **love**.
Children are complex, but they're not that
complicated.
They are little people with real feelings, thoughts and
Ideas. They are honest, and will remain that
Way if you give them guidance, structure,
And wise counsel.
They desire your attention,
Need nurturing and consistent
Instruction. But, more than anything,
Children thrive on genuine **love**.

Show Them Nothing but "Love"

Understanding what "Love is:"

Love Is . . .

Love is more than just a 4-letter word.
Love is a hug, and a kiss
It's a reassuring nod

Love is felt, seen, heard,
Love's pulse pounds from the heart
It is witnessed without words in your presence.

Love is sincere. It's full of hope.
Love is honest and true,
It's refreshingly real
Love is never giving up on you

Love is patient and kind,
Love listens
Love waits its turn
. . .Is always there to give a hand

Love is being the first to forgive
And being considerate of others
Love always gives a hand up
. . .Never leaves you alone.

Love is more than just saying I love you
It's saying and doing everything you promised.
Love's a daily demonstration. It's in the tone of your
voice, It's in the movement of your hands,
It's in kind deeds of choice

Love is unconditional; simple, pure and sweet.
It offers security, provides support; it cast out fear.
Love makes all the difference.
For love is understanding, and being there,
year after year, after year.

Now that's "love."

~

The Basics

Children need the basics. They need to feel safe and have structure, to become productive human beings. What they see (at home) is what they'll do. What they hear is what they'll say. Sometimes you may be wrong and your child right. Just be honest enough to admit it, so he (she) won't be confused.

~

Ethics Can't Be Taught

If you want your child to be ethical, be the example.
If you want your child to live by a higher standard,
You must live by that higher standard.
Be consistent with your instruction.
Don't adjust your decision to
Accommodate (your child).*
Always respect self and others.
Always demand respect in return.
Walk in unconditional love at
School, at home and
in public too.

"Mommie" Note: Sometimes I was too tired from my workday to reinforce an instruction. This only weakened my position of authority as a parent. You have to take a stand. And stand firm!

On Being Responsible:

A responsible parent provides for their child's basic needs, and gives the extras in moderation. Let your child earn the luxury items. It will increase their sense of value. They will have a greater appreciation for the little things in life. Teach your children to be committed. Give them chores. Consistency in instruction provides stability.

On Respect:

If you respect others,
You can demand respect in return.
Train your children to respect authority.
Teach your children to have respect for one another.
Practice good manners in all of your conversations.
Talk to your children every day. Talk, don't rattle.
There is a difference.
Have family talk, encourage the conversation exchange. But, also take time to laugh and have a good time together. Drop everything and listen when your children are sharing. You need to know what's on their mind.

On Being an Example

It helped to have a strong faith;
It was something I could lean on when times
were tough. It helped to be able to pray.
Somehow I knew everything would be alright.
It helped to be able to keep a song in my heart.
Sometimes I'd change the words to fit my spiritual
need. It helped me to be able to forgive before I
went to bed. It meant I could wake up with an
untainted heart. It helped to walk in unconditional

"love."

It meant looking only for the good in everyone I met.

"Mommie" Note: Mom - if you want to produce a lady,
be a lady at all times. To the Dads reading this: If you
want your son to be a man, be his best example of a man.

Everyday a life is being shaped by a
mother's love.

The **Art** of Good Communication

TALK, TALK, TALK!

"TEACH" – but, please don't lecture me

And please, PLEASE – "DON'T PREACH!!!"

Ps. I'm just sayin' speak in a calm, peaceful voice.

On Communicating with Your Child. . .

It's important to keep the doors of communication open with each one of your children. They need to know that they can talk to you about anything (everything). And when they open up the door of communication and begin to share with you:

1. Remember to listen attentively as they speak.
2. Look them in the eye to let them know that you are tuned in.
3. Get all of the facts. Get as much of the detail, without interrupting your child.
4. Remain calm, even when you feel like you want to scream.
5. Keep your voice soft and low.
6. Give your child the assurance that everything is going to be alright (because it is, now that you're involved).
7. Build confidence through words of faith and hope.
8. Establish stability by showing consistent support.
9. Maintain trust.
10. Offer the reassurance of your love.

Another way to keep the channel of communication open is to praise your children (child), often, for all of the good things that they do. Let's talk about the "praise," because praise can make a big difference in the parent/child relationship.

Praise! - Just Can't Get Enough

When your children take a stand for what is right,
Applaud them. If your child stands alone to be right
~~ Offer praise with rewards. ~~
Praise your children for every good thing they do.
Chores, homework, kindness toward others.
Good sportsmanship. Diligence. Give them praise.
Always offer praise for a job well done.
It will build character and self-esteem.
It will help them to become confident and
Responsible, while encouraging a sense
Of independence and self-worth.

"Mommie" note: Most children don't get enough praise. So, we have made a list of 100 phrases to help every parent get their praise on! Are you ready? :)

It's All about the Praise!

(You can do more with a praise than you can with a shout.)

When your child does a great job, give him/her praise. "Parental praise" will encourage your child to do more and help him become better at what he does. Praise builds self-esteem, keeps their thoughts elevated and strengthens character.

Children, who receive lots of praise, tend to have pleasant dispositions. Shouting, on the other hand, seems to yield a more aggressive personality type, and shouting is not good for your vocal chords.

Avoid the shout if you can - I know **you can** do it. :)

Since praise does wonders for every child, here are 100 ways you can praise your children every day:

That's phenomenal!! Great job!! I'm so proud of you! Terrific! Fantastic work!! That's incredible! Excellent!! Unbelievable work! Outstanding performance!! You've done a fantastic job!! Great work! Your being honest means so much to me!

We're proud of you! I love you because you are wonderful! You are a good girl (boy)! Try it one more time! You almost got it that time! That's fantastic!! You are talented!! That's great!! You can do it! Great

89

effort, keep trying!!! You're making progress! Thank you. You are a big help!

You do great work! I'm absolutely impressed!! Awesome! Congratulations!! You won! You did it! Good job! Keep it up! Outstanding job! How thoughtful! How nice!! What a great idea! I am so excited for you!! How wonderful!

How beautiful! Your work is superb! Great! You've earned it! I know you can do it!! Keep trying, you're almost there! This is absolutely gorgeous! You did it without any help! Keep up the good work!! How nice of you to do that! How nice of you to do that! This is remarkable!

Oh, how beautiful! Magnificent! This is so beautiful!! You did a fine job!! I'm so thankful to have you for a son!! How wonderful to have you for a daughter! Your work is outstanding! You are brilliant! Wow! You've really grown up!! Thanks for helping and showing that you care!!

You've earned my respect! You're my shining star! You've got what it takes!! I knew you could do it! You should be proud of yourself! That's a great idea!! You're a genius!! What an imagination! What talent! You made all the difference!

You're doing a lot better! Great answer! Fantastic response! You are No. 1!! Thanks for trying! You're getting there! Remarkable! You're a real trooper!! You're unique, and that's good!! Your work is unbelievable!! Very good!!

You are so kind! You are a winner! That's very impressive! You deserve a big hug! What effort!! Yea!! - You did it!! Good for you!! Thank you for being honest!! You are a great example for others!! You've got what it takes to succeed! You have sensational talent!! You have made us proud!!!

Your help made a difference!! What a wonderful friend you are! (referring to a friendship with peers) Your project is amazing!! It is exceptional! YES!!! :) The time you invested really made a difference!! Thank you for being a blessing!!! What a great idea!!! You are a joy to be around!!

Some phrases were taken from The Positive Line #79930, Item CS-737

"Mommie? . . . Can you hear me now?"

I've Got Questions

I've got questions, Mom.
Can you help me think this through?
How do we know when right is right
Or if there's something we shouldn't do?

Sometimes you can't hear me
Because I don't always speak out loud.
(But), I just need to know you love me
And that I'm a desired child.

Can you look in my eyes and see
The 'trouble that's troubling' me?
Sometimes I just need a hug
Or to hear you say a kind word to me.

I love you Mom, but it's tough out here,
There must be a better way.
I feel like everything I did was wrong
In how I handled yesterday.

I guess I just need some guidance
And to know I'll make it through.
Who do you call on when things are tough,
When you don't know what to do?

  ". . .Looking for answers."

"Special" Mommie note:

Mommie, are you listening? Do you talk with your children every day? Do you take the time to listen to what they have to say?

Please don't take for granted that things are going fine, when your child needs to have a conversation and you don't have the time.

Oh, we know that you're busy, that you barely have time for you. But, when it comes to good communication, Mom, you've got a job to do!

"Mommie" to "Mommy"

"Mommie" Note: Some mornings my Mom made fresh squeezed orange juice, eggs, smothered potatoes with onions, and more. She put lots of love into everything she did and always made us feel special. But, more importantly, she was a Proverbs 31 woman. (Read Proverbs 31: 1 - 31.) She lived a life of virtue and taught us to do the same.

The ANSWER

The world is looking for answers.
Parents don't quite know what to do.
But Jesus is the answer.
He was for me, and He can be for you.

Ask me about Him,
I can lead you to Him today.
For Jesus is the answer,
Jesus is the way.

He is the way, the truth, the light.
He will help you do what's right.
You can call on Him any time of day,
Morning, noon or night.

Learn to love like Jesus loves,
And seek the will of the Father above,
As you learn to love unconditionally.
He'll provide protection and security.

~

May I show you the way?

"A Special Kind of Mommy"

There's something special about a woman who has a reverence for God. But, there's something extra special about a Mom who spends quality time with her children and raises them in the fear and admonition of the Lord.

Let your children know that Jesus loves them, and that He came to give them life in abundance, with nothing missing or broken. He is your safety net from all trouble, if you put your trust in Him. To trust God is to accept Jesus as Lord and Savior of your life.

Sometimes your toddler only needs a diaper change or two. At times your school-aged boy or girl may need an explanation of a rule.

Motherhood is a job with tremendous rewards, if you are willing to give it your all, your best; like staying up late to help them study, to make sure they pass the test.

Motherhood means listening and loving and being available when you're needed most; and preparing eggs and pancakes for breakfast, instead of just serving toast.

It's reading a bed-time story and tucking them into bed real tight; listening to their prayers and assuring them of your love, before you say good night.

A Great New Beginning:

You can invite Jesus to come into your heart today. Ask Him to save you and cleanse you from unrighteousness, and from sins, both known and unknown. As you repent of your sins and confess Jesus as Lord of your life, you'll have the assurance of spending eternity with Him.

Read 1 John 1:9, and Romans 10:9 aloud to establish your relationship with Jesus Christ and to begin a new and victorious life, filled with peace and joy.

Did you just pray the prayer of salvation and make Jesus Lord of your life? Congratulations! This is the most important decision of you could ever make. And the angels in heaven are rejoicing at this very moment, for heaven just became your eternal home.

Not only does this decision change your future residence, but, Jesus will help you be a better Mom, make better decisions, and become your constant companion and friend if you ask Him to.

Worship God together as a family. Live a life of shalom – fully satisfied; completely whole; and enjoy a state of wellness; peaceful, with nothing missing, nothing broken.

"Mommy Tweets"

(from one Mommie to another)

"What is your child saying? Please remove the barriers and communicate!!!"

"When your children are speaking listen attentively!"

"Talk to your babies, and toddlers too. Establish good communication before they go to school."

"Silence is another form of communication - what is your child not saying?"

"If your children are not communicating verbally, check their body language; notice their behavior."

"Is your child speaking? Listen quietly. Talk – softly. . . .and let the phone ring."

"Don't hold back – tell them what they need to know. Share good information, it will help them grow."

"You are your child's first educator. Why not give them a jump start? Training begins at home."

"Have meaningful conversations every day."

"Hey Mom, Your Children are calling! . . .and that teenager in a crisis, is refusing to go to school. Can you Stop! . . . just for a minute?

Your children need YOU."

Surviving Motherhood, to Reap the Benefits

~ from feeling overwhelmed to overwhelming joy ~

Moms, like everyone else will experience "trial and error," have good days and days that aren't as good; victorious moments, and what may seem like an occasional defeat. But, for the Mom on a mission, the appearance of defeat is only temporary. The not-so-good days will be overturned, and the errors will be corrected.

During these more challenging moments of motherhood, you may have to encourage yourself and become your own cheering squad. Just know that joy will come in the morning.

Only when you reach the point where your diligence and hard work have connected to form the outline of your child's character, and when you see your child becoming that noble person you've been chiseling on, will you begin to fill (up) with joy on the inside.

One by one, your children will grow up. The growth process may seem slow at first; then, suddenly they're grown and gone. And, if you've done a good job, one by one they'll return to say "Thank you, Mom."

"Good Morning Mommie"

I'm a baby now, and there's not a lot I can do.

But, when I get older,

Theses are the things I'll remember about you.

How you woke up early each morning

Always in a great mood.

How you took time to talk with me

And serve the best of food.

Mommy, you are the greatest,

I'm so blessed that I've got you.

Mommy dear, is there anything,

Anything that I can do for you?

Love, Your "baby" (for now)

Thanks Mom

Thanks, Mom, for all those talks we had - made a difference. Now I use pure thoughts to reason. Today I apply common sense. Thanks for loving me Mom, and for all you continue to do. I'm happy for the time we had. I'm so glad I could talk with you.

I love you Mom, and I still need you. But, I'm a lot older now, as you can see. All I want is to make you proud of me. For now I understand all the sacrifices that you made for me. *"Your High School Graduate"*

It's Never Too Late

I have a young adult now. There are times when I feel I didn't share enough, or give enough good information or advice. There are things that I understand today, that I didn't understand/know then.

You can't share what you don't know, or give advice on something for which you have no knowledge. So, what can you do about it now? Pray over it and look for creative ways to share good information in an advisory-friendly-way.

Each of us, adults and children too, receive communication differently. Tune into your child's preferred "communication zone." And ask God to reveal to you the things you need to know.

In "The Five Love Languages," author, Gary Chapman shares the five common love languages of mankind. They are:

1. Words of Affirmation
2. Acts of Service
3. Receiving Gifts
4. Quality Time
5. Physical Touch

Some people respond well to positive words of praise and "words of affirmation," while some are driven by "acts of service," and are very responsive to those who serve them.

Then there are those who enjoy "receiving gifts." A token of appreciation will motivate this person to action. "Quality time" is another love language. This person places more value on the quality of time you spend with them than on gifts or material things.

The fifth love language category is "physical touch." Hugs can do wonders for this person, for they respond well/need to have physical contact. Most children respond well to hugs.

Knowing your child's love language, improves communication and allows you to have greater understanding and respect for each other. Now, if you're a Mom who feels that you may have missed it because your children are older, I want to encourage you. It's never too late.

As long as there is life and breath and a willing vessel, you can be instrumental in making positive changes to improve the relationship between you and your children. Ask God to help you, and trust Him to do just that.

The bond of motherhood should never be broken. Even when your children are grown - and on their own - they still need your prayers and words of encouragement.

Now that I have your attention, I have just one question: **"Mommie, R U Listening???"**

Here's what worked for me: During the course of each workday I learned to, to take some "Me Time" to refresh both mind and spirit. I encourage you to do the same. You will need to Stop!! whatever you're doing, and enter into a period of rest from your work. Just 5 or 10 minutes can make a big difference.

Next, Breathe!! Inhale deeply. Meditate on anything positive, like your last vacation, a day at the spa, or the promises in God's Word. His promises will strengthen you. Now take another deep breath. Fill your lungs with oxygen, and inhale those thoughts. Be invigorated, filled with strength. Exhale. Repeat twice.

Now Listen!! Listen, first to your inner spirit, as you tune out the noise around you. Hear what your spirit is saying, as you think on things that are lovely, on things that are pure, and of a good report, thoughts of kindness, and things of virtue. Continue to refresh your mind, allowing all negative thoughts to escape.

God has given us many promises in His Word (The Holy Bible). He wants us to be encouraged, and to encourage others. One way to receive to do that is to meditate on His Word and to apply His promises to your daily lives. Here is a selection of verses to choose from:

These promises kept me encouraged:

"I can do all things through Christ who strengthens me" (Philippians 4:13). Today, I receive your strength.

"In His presence is fullness of joy" (Psalm 66:11).* I'm going to stay in your presence Lord. :)

"The joy of the Lord is my strength" (Nehemiah 8:10b).

"I will trust in the Lord forever, for in the Lord God is everlasting strength" (Isaiah 26:4).

"He will keep me in perfect peace as I keep my mind stayed on Him." (Refer to Isaiah 26:3).

"Love never fails. Therefore, today and every day I will love unconditionally."   (Reference: 1 Corinthians 13:8; 1 John 4: 7) I'm going to love like you love.

"I know that you will never leave me, nor forsake me, for you are my God" (Reference: Hebrews 13:5b).

*I kept this one on my desk.

Meditate on the promise and believe that you can have what it says, and teach your children to do the same. It really helps to personalize it. (See below.)

"I am so thankful Lord that you never change. Jesus, You are the same, yesterday, today and forever." (Reference: Malachi 3:6; Hebrews 13:8)

"I will not concentrate on the mean-spirited people, or on anyone who does evil, for I know you will take care of them for me for you said vengeance belongs to you. Therefore, I will lean on, rely on, and put my trust in You" (Reference: Colossians 3:2, Romans 12:19).

"I will not have fear, because you are always with me I will not be disenchanted, upset or stressed, because You are my God. I draw from your strength Lord, for I know that you are helping me. And I thank you for holding me up against all odds and embracing me with your unfailing love" (Refer to: Isaiah 41:10).

"Lord, You are my refuge and strength, a very present help when I'm troubled." (Scriptures from Psalm 46:1) Thank you for helping me.

"I will trust in You with all of my heart, and lean totally on You." (Reference: Proverbs 3:5)

"I will think on things that are lovely and just, honest and pure, things of truth, virtue and of a good report. And I will give you praise," (Refer to: Philippians 4:8b).

"I am thankful today for your peace which surpasses all understanding, and keeps my heart and mind on You Lord. Shalom. (Refer to: Philippians 4:7)

~ You'll know the right things to do, if you remain quiet long enough to think things through. Inner peace starts from within and remains there.

Remember to: Stop! Breathe!! and Listen!!!

Our "Words of Wisdom" to You

(These "Words of Wisdom" are spoken in love.)

The following words of wisdom come from eleven mothers, grandmothers and/or mentor moms who raised their children and youth to be outstanding citizens, making a difference in the world.

"Love!! Give them love. Children need love."

Regina Engelhardt

"Love, encouragement, guidance and structure is what children need."   Gail Perry-Mason, Mom

"God has given us this special privilege to be a mother to our children; so let's not take it lightly. Too many of us are "friending" our children, and missing out on the godly task God has given us of nurturing, loving, guiding, and disciplining."   Betty Tanner

"God gives all of our children gifts; as parents we have to help them open and nurture those gifts."

G. Perry-Mason, Mom

"My mission is - and has been - to make sure that my children turn out to be the kind of people that I would like to have as friends, who deserves good friends in return. Today, they are two beautiful people that I would want to get to know if I were to meet them for the first time."   Amina Fakir, Mom

"Give your children lots of love. Love is the key to opening up doors to their heart."

Sandra Williams, Grandmother

"Build your children up from the day you see them. Never call them bad names or say 'bad girl' or 'bad boy' to your children. Learn to correct your child without saying negative words. Regina Engelhardt, Grandmother

"Hug your child more and say "I love you." A child who receives lots of hugs and love words is a more secure child." Sharon Dumas

"I am "Team Mommie," and I am on the cheer team for my children." Gail Perry-Mason, Mom

"I prayed specific and detailed prayers for my children in utero, and still do so to this day. When my prayers are answered, my children share in my joy and my faith. The faith we shared when they were small children has blossomed into a mighty work in both of their lives." Amina Fakir, Mom

"The time spent with my children when they were young, attending their activities and being an involved parent, was precious time. Suddenly, they were grown and now my husband and I have plenty of time to do whatever we want."
Mn. Deborah Dixson, Grandmother

"Our children will meet many people. They will choose some of those people to be their friends. So, they don't need us to be friends; they need us to be mothers! An awesome task, but God chose us. So let's not fail!" Betty Tanner, Grandmother

"I raised my children to have faith in God. Now they have faith; they are strong and they value others."
Maeolia Snider, Grandmother

"It's very important to pray for your children, but it's also important to pray with them. I noticed a major difference when I did. On those days that we prayed together, my children always had positive outcomes, and they could hardly wait to come home and share their experiences with me." Lucille Moore, Grandmother

"Keeping God first, cannot be overemphasized? We cannot ask our children to put God first if they don't see us doing so." Amina Fakir, Mom

"Everyday my sons and I are students in this life, . . .I am always open to learn from my sons. They've taught me so much about life." Gail Perry-Mason

Our family learned to live two wage-levels below what we could financially afford, which allowed me the option to work part-time, or be a stay-at-home Mom. You can do it! Mn. Deborah Dixson

"As a grandmother and book coach, I encouraged my granddaughter to publish her story when I realized that she loved to write. Her first book was published when she was eight years old. She is leaving a legacy." Mn. Mary Edwards, Grandmother

"It is an honor to get on my knees with my sons, because now they help me get back up as I lift them up in prayer. We must make sure we pray with our children daily." Gail Perry-Mason, Mother

"You may not agree on all things, but try to understand. Always let your children know that you will be there for them, and that you are available to talk about anything. Then, seek God for wisdom and understanding on all things." Sandra Williams

"I often recall what my dear friend said to me before my son was born. "You can put the time in when they're young, or you can put the time in when they're older, and in trouble. Either way, they're going to get a chunk of your life." Amina Fakir, Mom

"Teach your children and grandchildren the importance of leaving a legacy. Let them start early. It will help them to understand who they are. Legacy-Leaving Each Generation A Chronicle of You."
Mn. Mary Edwards, Grandmother

"When the children were growing up, my husband and I would spend the first 15 minutes after he arrived home from work sharing about our day. We exchanged information over a cup of tea. This activity strengthened and enhanced our marriage bond well after the children left our nest."
Mn. Deborah Dixson, Grandmother

These Words of Wisdom are from:

Mn. Deborah Dixson, Mother (3), grandmom
Sharon Dumas, Mentor (Mom)
Regina Engelhardt, Mother (3 daughters), grandmom
Mn. Mary Edwards, Mom, grandmom
Amina Fakir, Mom (2)
Gail Perry-Mason, Mom (3 sons)
Lucille Moore, Mom (4), grandmom
Maeolia Snider, Mom (3), grandmom
Betty Tanner, Mom (1 son), grandmom
Sandra Williams, Mom, grandmom

{Moms have son(s) and daughter(s), where not specified}

Working - Married Moms

Love, love, love your husband. Children need to see their parents respecting and showing each other love in word and deed. Love, respect and responsibility are all a part of the marriage-bond (glue) when it comes to children and the family unit. You are their example for when they become adults.

From time to time, encourage your husband to share in some of the traditional "Mommie chores," like grocery shopping, moderate housework, and cooking the main course for dinner. Think about it: Did you ever see "superwoman" with a family and all of the other responsibilities too? :)

Besides, it can be fun having Dad in the kitchen. You'd be surprised at how good his specialty dishes are. Don't forget to give complements and show gratitude for his labor of love. Praise works wonders for Dad too. :)

Be sure to coordinate the responsibilities at home so that the whole family is working together. Working together can also include teaching your children to help their siblings once they've completed their task, if that sibling still has a lot to do. It's so beautiful to see every member of the family working together to make the family work. It is a bond that cannot be broken.

"...Let us love one another: for love is of God. . ."

(1 John 4:7)

A Word to Single Moms

I use the term, "single Mom," with the utmost respect. For so often, single Moms are not respected, not appreciated and seldom are the recipients of unconditional love.

Mom, if you know that your child's father is a very good Dad, and desires to have a strong role in your child's life, please work out your differences so that your child has quality time with him. Children need their Dads too. It was ordained by God. Dads provide protection and security in a natural way. It's difficult enough for children not to have physical access to both Mom and Dad every day.

One word to the wise woman with children, never degrade or bash your child's father in the presence of your child. If you cannot exonerate, edify or uplift his character, then it is better to remain silent.

Learn to respect one another despite any differences you might have. Have respect for one another in front of the children because they are watching; and have respect even when the children are not around. It's so much healthier to get along and be at peace, to have "shalom."

"Shalom" - is the God-kind of peace where nothing is missing in your life and nothing is broken. You are content, and in harmony with His Divine plan for your life.

. . .to Our Dads!

So many fathers are missing in action and for so many different reasons. Whether he's on active duty in the armed forces, had to relocate for his job, is suffering from a long-term illness, lacks commitment, incarcerated, or being controlled by chemical substances; children have a great desire to communicate with their Father, and to know that 'Daddy cares.' It just comes naturally.

Pray for the fathers who have little to no involvement in their children's lives. Pray for Dad's everywhere.

God's plan was for husbands and wives to love each other, and for homes to be filled with love, children and laughter.

Special note: Children are very sensitive about the absent parent and that parent who is seldom there. If you can't make favorable comments about the absent parent, it is better not to say anything at all. (Read it again until you get it.) Remember, we are loving unconditionally. :)

To all of the Dads out there: We love you; and we're praying for you.

"Pray without ceasing" (1 Thessalonians 5:17).

Grand-Mommy, Did You Get My Text?

Ps. I'm waiting to hear from you. . .

To all the 21st Grand-Mommies raising grandchildren, especially those Grand-Mommies who haven't quite connected with social media, or found a level of comfort with "modern technology;" these next few pages were written in "love" with "you" in mind.

DO YOU REMEMBER WHEN
There Was No **Technology?**
An Outcry from the baby boomers.

(Dedicated to baby boomers and grandparents.)

Technology has changed our world. Our society looks the same, but does not respond in the same ways it did twenty or thirty years ago, for that matter even six months ago. Technological advancements have connected the world and made us one big family of instant communicators across the globe.

Just as the earth is spinning on its axis, faster than we can imagine or feel, so too is technology propelling us into the next phase of life. As the earth's axis is to the earth, technology is to man.

Where it used to take months to transact business across the world, it now takes seconds, through one of many mediums or multiple streams. We have seen the introduction of information technology (IT) and information systems; major advancements, enhancements or improvements in technology on every level. (Yes, the Jetsons' era is here.)

Today we connect via Skype to see the person we're talking to. We've gone from telegraph to telephone, from telephone to facsimile, and from faxing to a wireless generation of computers and cell phones; from U.S. mail to Fed Ex, from magnetic, tack, and self-adhesive bulletin boards to Pinterest (posting them electronically) and Insta-gram.

We send electronic mail (email), text messages, and have become as comfortable with e-commerce shopping as retail shopping at the mall. We have moved from our private spaces to an open book with face – "Facebook", from (being) Linked-in to a tweet - "Twitter."

There was a time when it was acceptable to check voice mail whenever you got home, now you're expected to respond instantly to every text.

Oh hear the 'Baby Boomer's Cry:' "You used to call and leave a message. Now you call, text, page and email me; try to link me in, Facebook and tweet me, then wonder why you can't reach me. Well, I'm still here, trying to stay connected. I'm just so busy trying to respond to all of those messages from you and everybody else."

Will somebody just call me please???? And this time will you leave just one message, and give me at least until tomorrow to call you back?"

Technology Tip: No one will know how much you don't know until you tell them. Always try to learn something new, and learn as much as you can. Knowledge is power. And remember, technology really is a good thing, after all, where would we be without it? **:)**

p.s. Grandma:
Just relax! And know that everything's gonna' be alright. ☺

"Grand Mommy" Note: Be encouraged. We feel it too. Stay encouraged, because your grandchildren need you!

~

"Stress Remedies"

because You deserve a break today!

~

Stress Relievers for the Working Mom --> at work

Common Symptoms of Stress:

▪ Frequent headaches, neck ache, back pain, muscle spasms
▪ Light headedness, faintness, dizziness, problems swallowing, dry mouth,
▪ Heartburn, stomach pain, nausea, hiccups, excessive belching, flatulence, constipation, diarrhea,
▪ Difficulty breathing, sighing,
▪ Worry, guilt, nervousness, frustration, depression, frequent mood swings,
▪ Increased or decreased appetite, insomnia, disturbing dreams,
▪ Difficulty learning new information, forgetfulness, disorganization, difficulty in making decisions,
▪ Feels overloaded, overwhelmed, unable to concentrate, has little self-worth, poor punctuality,
▪ Extreme tiredness, fatigue, weakness, problems in communication, isolation from others, . . .(This is a partial list of symptoms of stress.)

Yes, stress affects many key body systems, including the nervous system, cardiovascular, respiratory, endocrine, musculoskeletal and gastrointestinal systems.

Taken from the 50 Common Signs and Symptoms of Stress, The American Institute of Stress

"Stress Remedies"

Stressed out?? Stop Everything!!! ➔ (Location: Find a quiet area – such as a Ladies Lounge)

Remedy: Close your eyes, and call a "time out." ➔ Now take a deep breath ➔ as you fill your mind with pleasant thoughts ➔ breathe deeply ➔ do nothing for five minutes ➔ and smile from the inside –out as you open your eyes.

~

It's Mid-day, and you're feeling a little tense . . . (Location: same as above)

Remedy: Take deep breath, lift your hands above your head and stretch slowly. Fill the pull, while stretching as far as you can go. Stretch upward toward the right, lean and hold. Hold it for 10 seconds. Next do the same stretch toward the left and hold 10 seconds. If you are sitting, you can also stretch leaning back, and hold. Take another deep breath, exhale and feel better. Repeat at least twice. Notice how much stronger you feel. ☺

~

Had a "tough day at work" and now it's time to go home. (Your office/workstation)

Remedy: "Take five." You can begin this exercise at the close of your workday. In an upright posture, position yourself comfortably in your work chair. While sitting tall, take a series of deep breaths with eyes closed. Don't move, until you are totally relaxed. Sit for a moment and enjoy the comforts of your stress-free work area. It's time for self-love; love on yourself.

~

If you are still stressed when you get to your vehicle, after a long day at work, do the following. (Before you drive away)

Remedy: Put on some soft, soothing music to drive to. Take a deep breath and hold as you warm the car.

~

Need to calm your thoughts or stop worrying about things? . . . . (Do this daily)

Remedy: Find a promise in the Word of God that you can stand on each day. Focus on that promise; meditate on it, and keep those Words visible throughout the day. Now, "only believe" (Luke 8:50).

~

Final "Mommie" note: I was so caught up from my work day I couldn't hear him speak. He was used to repeating it once or twice, but on this particular day, my son had repeated it thrice. On this day my son said to me, "Mommie, you aren't listening!!!" And with great disappointment, he turned around sadly and walked away. That is when I knew I needed to make some changes in how I handled my work-day stress.

"Mom, you can do it too!"

Sharing is Love in Action:

Maybe you know another Mom, or have a friend who is struggling with the responsibilities of motherhood. This book could make the difference in her life.

Or maybe her child has come face-to-face with a bully regularly. So many lives have been lost, because parents and children were not informed about bully prevention.

You can be proactive about bully prevention by sharing information like this with other Moms. Let's work together to stop the bullying, to preserve future generations.

Kindly share the information about our books and resources with others. Buy a copy to share with a family who can't afford it, or consider giving this book away, just because you care.

Ps. You have my permission to share it on Facebook. ☺

More books by Patrice Lee:

"...Overcome Every Obstacle . . . and Land on Top"
"Bully Me? . . .NO MORE! ! !" (3rd – 6th grade)
"Bully Me?. . .NO MAS! ! !" (Spanish Translation)
"Bully Me? . . . Oh NO!!!" a TEEN Resource
"Tips" & "Tools" for a Safe and Healthy School Year
"Happy to be Me!" (preschool – 2nd grade)
"Daddy! . . .Can You Hear Me???"

To order additional books go to:

www.Leep4Joy.com

If the local store in your area doesn't have this book visible, please ask for it. If it isn't available yet, kindly ask them to contact us. Your inquiry may help save a child's life from the negative effects of being bullied or the fears associated with it.

Patrice Lee continues to write and publish books. She speaks to corporations, youth groups, at conferences, and seminars; and facilitates workshops for K-12 students, teachers and parent organizations.

If this book has helped you in any way please share your comments with us: ucantbullyme@gmail.com

About the Author:

As a young mother, Patrice Lee had many responsibilities and wore many hats, from a very demanding full-time job, to caregiver (caring for loved ones) and serving as guardian for those family members who were ill. Author Lee had to learn very quickly how to juggle those responsibilities and manage stress.

Though she experienced excessive bullying as an adult, Lee began each day with a smile, a positive attitude and a willingness to do and be her best. Through a message of faith, hope, love and laughter she helps moms manage stress so they can enjoy the positive rewards of motherhood.

www.Leep4Joy.com

A book created for every woman, color, race, creed, and ethnicity - from all walks of life, because "motherhood" is common ground between us.

www.ingramcontent.com/pod-product-compliance
Lightning Source LLC
Chambersburg PA
CBHW062144020426
42334CB00020B/2501